FORMS OF GOVERNMENT

BY PETER BENOIT

D0107416

CHILDREN'S PRESS®

An Imprint of Scholastic Inc.

New York   Toronto   London   Auckland   Sydney
Mexico City   New Delhi   Hong Kong
Danbury, Connecticut

BRINGING HISTORY to LIFE

Cover: Winston Churchill (right), the prime minister of the United Kingdom (a constitutional monarchy); Franklin D. Roosevelt (center), the president of the United States (a republic); and Joseph Stalin (left), the general secretary of the Soviet Union (a Communist nation), meet to discuss the way Europe would be governed in the aftermath of World War II.

Consultant
James Marten, PhD
Professor and Chair, History Department
Marquette University
Milwaukee, Wisconsin

Library of Congress Cataloging-in-Publication Data
Benoit, Peter, 1955–
 Forms of government / by Peter Benoit.
 pages cm — (Cornerstones of Freedom.)
 Includes bibliographical references and index.
 ISBN 978-0-531-21330-8 (lib. bdg.) — ISBN 978-0-531-25826-2 (pbk.)
 1. Comparative government—Juvenile literature. 2. State, The—Juvenile literature. 3. Political science—Juvenile literature. 4. United States—Politics and government—Juvenile literature. I. Title.
 JF51.B45 2014
 320.3—dc23   2013021559

1 2 3 4 5 6 7 8 9 10 R 23 22 21 20 19 18 17 16 15 14

Photographs ©: age fotostock/Everett Collection: 46; AP Images: 38 (Charles Tasnadi), 15 (Jonathan J. Cooper), 10, 13 (North Wind Picture Archives), 19 (Vahid Salemi), 34; Bridgeman Art Library/National Army Museum, London: 11; Dreamstime: 5 top, 35 (giuliachristin); Franklin D. Roosevelt Presidential Library/flickr: cover; Getty Images: 22 (AFP), 48 (Carl Iwasaki/Time & Life Pictures), 27 (Catherine Henriette/AFP), 17 (Mandel Ngan/AFP), 18 (Michael Fein/Bloomberg), 32 (Ramzi Haidar/AFP); iStockphoto: 5 top, 12 (DNY59), 51, 59 (jcarillet), 14, 56 top (wynnter); Landov/KCNA/EPA: 23; Media Bakery: 8 (Hill Street Studios), back cover (Rob Melnychuk); Newscom/Scott J. Ferrell/Congressional Quarterly: 42; Reuters: 49 (Charles Platiau), 28 (Fahad Shadeed), 4 bottom, 29 (Geoff Pugh/Pool), 50, 57 (Grigory Dukor), 44 (Jason Reed), 4 top, 45 (Kevin Lamarque KL/ME), 31 (Paul Hanna), 24, 56 bottom (Rafael Perez); Superstock, Inc.: 55 (Ambient Images Inc.), 47 (Everett Collection), 26 (Justin Guariglia/age fotostock), 37 (Underwood Photo Archives), 6; The Image Works: 41 (Baileys Archive/africanpictures), 54 (Jon Burbank), 7 (Nurun Nahar Nargish/Drik/Majority World), 2, 3, 20, 36 (RIA-Novosti).

Maps by XNR Productions, Inc.

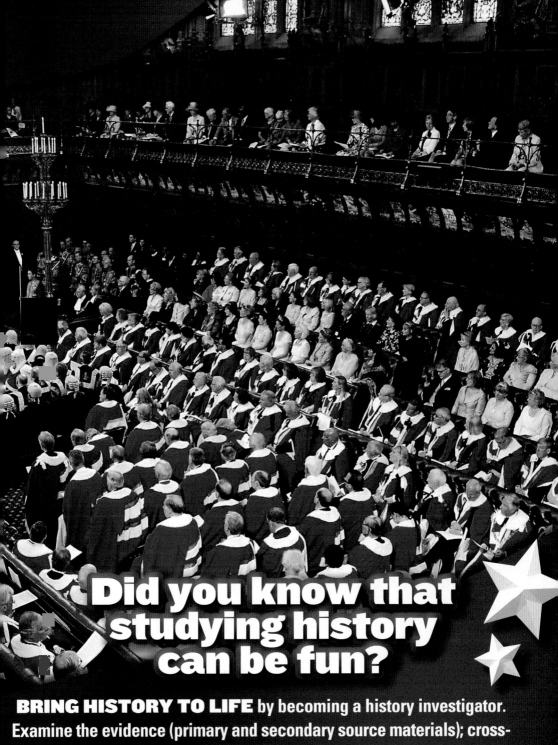

Did you know that studying history can be fun?

BRING HISTORY TO LIFE by becoming a history investigator. Examine the evidence (primary and secondary source materials); cross-examine the people and witnesses. Take a look at what was happening at the time—but be careful! What happened years ago might suddenly become incredibly interesting and change the way you think!

Contents

Making the Rules

In ancient Rome, government officials called senators worked together to create new laws for the Roman people.

Since the formation of the earliest human communities, people have made rules to keep order and promote the common good. Early societies chose leaders who were wise and strong enough to make and enforce those rules. As communities grew in size, different groups began to form within them. These smaller groups each

ROME WAS FOUNDED MORE

had their own ideas about how the society should work. This made leaders' jobs much more complicated. In many societies, these rulers began to share some of their authority with others. This allowed representatives of multiple groups to participate in making rules.

Today's governments face similar challenges. Different societies have values, goals, and histories that are unlike one another. As a result, many forms of government exist. Each has its own principles and laws. Two nations may organize their governments, direct their **economies**, or elect their leaders in very different ways. To understand the role that nations play in the larger world, it is important to examine how these different forms of government have developed over time and how they interact with one another.

Today, people in many countries around the world, including Bangladesh, choose their government leaders by voting in elections.

THAN 2,700 YEARS AGO.

CHAPTER 1

THE UNITED STATES GOVERNMENT

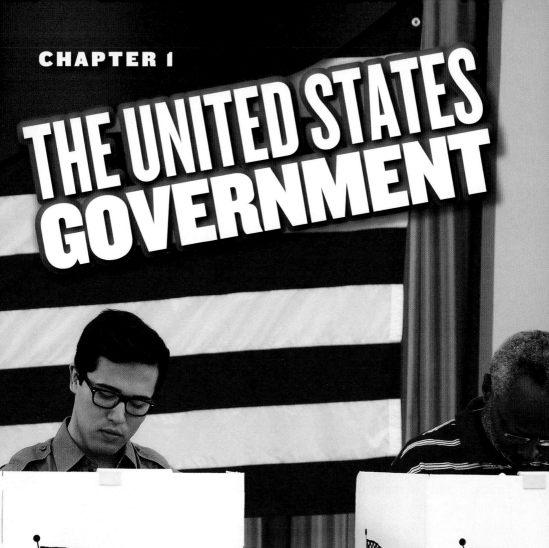

The first U.S. presidential election occurred in 1789. Since 1792 this election has been held every four years.

THE UNITED STATES USES A form of government known as a republic. This means that it is ruled by representatives who are chosen by the citizens of the country. The country's founders chose this form of leadership because they believed it was the fairest way of giving people a voice in the government.

In the United States, most leaders are chosen by voters in elections. The people influence the government by choosing leaders who share their opinions about how the country should be run. The U.S. government has limited control over the economy. Instead, most businesses are privately owned and operated by individuals and corporations.

In the Boston Tea Party, colonists protested a British tea tax by disguising themselves as Native Americans, boarding ships, and throwing the cargo of tea into Boston Harbor.

Seeking Independence

The United States was formed by a group of 13 British **colonies** in North America. The colonies were ruled by the British government. However, they did not get to elect representatives to Parliament, the British lawmaking body. Unhappy with the rule of the British government, the colonists decided to fight for a bigger role in their own leadership. Groups of colonists began staging protests against laws they believed to be unfair. Parliament responded by issuing new laws to punish them. Many colonists began calling for full independence from Great Britain.

In 1774, 56 **delegates** from 12 of the colonies met in Philadelphia, Pennsylvania, to form the First Continental Congress. They debated whether it was in the colonies' best interests to seek representation in Parliament or full independence. Before they could make a final decision, a group of colonists fought British soldiers at the Battles of Lexington and Concord on April 19, 1775. Three weeks later, the Second Continental Congress met in Philadelphia. It established a Continental army and attempted to reach a peace agreement with Great Britain. Britain refused, and all-out war seemed unavoidable. The following year, the Continental Congress issued the Declaration of Independence. This document officially stated that the colonies were no longer subject to British rule.

American colonists killed 273 British soldiers in the Battles of Lexington and Concord and lost 95 of their own men.

Soon after the Declaration of Independence was issued, the Continental Congress began to draft a document known as the Articles of Confederation. The Articles established limited powers of government for the Continental Congress. It could direct the war effort, engage in **diplomacy** with European countries, and resolve territorial disputes. However, it could not collect taxes or regulate the economy.

Upon declaring independence, the 13 colonies had become individual states. After winning the war against Great Britain in 1783, these states struggled to find common economic and political ground. The Continental Congress called for delegates from each state to meet in Philadelphia in 1787. There, they would replace the Articles by drafting a **constitution** for the United States.

Every year, Americans celebrate July 4 as Independence Day because it marks the anniversary of the adoption of the Declaration of Independence.

George Washington (center), a hero of the Revolutionary War, led the Constitutional Convention and was later chosen as the first president of the United States.

Choosing Leaders

Though the United States had fully established its independence when the war against Great Britain ended in 1783, its work had barely begun. Under the Articles of Confederation, the people could not elect national leaders. The national **legislature** could not make laws for the whole nation. During the summer of 1787, the 55 delegates at the Constitutional Convention debated how to make the new government fair for all the people.

Some delegates favored a powerful national government where the number of legislators from each state would be based on the state's population. Smaller states argued they would have no legislative power in such a government. They favored a system where each state had an equal number of legislators. Eventually a compromise was reached. Delegates agreed on a bicameral legislature. This meant that the legislature would be divided into two

YESTERDAY'S HEADLINES

Even before the Constitutional Convention, delegates were aware of the challenges facing them in forming a new government. In a letter dated April 16, 1787, delegate James Madison (above) of Virginia wrote of the importance of a strong national government. Madison feared that a weak national government would lead to the interests of larger states outweighing minority opinions. He also supported a system of checks and balances to guarantee that no one branch of government would become too strong. After the convention, Madison became a leading spokesman for the Constitution's **ratification.**

houses. For the House of Representatives, states with larger populations would elect more members. Those with smaller populations would elect fewer representatives. The other house was called the Senate. The delegates agreed that each state would elect two senators, regardless of its population.

The delegates also hammered out compromises on how best to elect a president and vice president. Eventually, they agreed to use a system of electors chosen by state legislatures. The number of electors assigned to each state would be based on population. Once chosen, the electors would cast their votes in presidential elections.

The delegates determined that each state would be able to decide for itself who was allowed to vote in elections. As a result, women and enslaved people throughout the nation were barred from voting for many years. Generally, only white property-owning males at least 21 years of age could choose the electors who, in turn, selected the president and vice president. Today, all citizens over the age of 18 can vote. However, the practice of using electors to choose the president and vice president persists almost unchanged since it was put in place by the Constitutional Convention.

In a republic like the United States, voters choose representatives who lead the government. Those representatives are elected individually for a set term in office. Presidents serve four-year terms and can only be

Presidential electors from each state take an oath of office before casting their votes.

elected two times. Representatives serve two-year terms, while senators serve six-year terms. There are no limits on how many times a congressperson can be elected.

Balancing Power

The delegates remembered the absolute power the British government had held over the colonies. As a result, they feared giving too much power to the president and vice president. Instead, they divided the government's power among three branches: the executive branch, the legislative branch, and the judicial branch.

The three branches' powers are controlled by a system of checks and balances. This means that no one branch is more powerful than another. The executive branch, headed by the president, enforces laws. The legislative branch, or Congress, can introduce plans for new laws, called bills, but the president's agreement is required to sign them into law. The Supreme Court, head of the judicial branch, decides whether those laws agree with the Constitution.

The delegates spread out power not only among the three branches of the federal government, but also between federal and state governments. Such compromise was necessary if the Constitution was to be approved by the individual state legislatures. Some states worried that the federal government had too much power. Others felt the balance was fair, and they ratified the Constitution quickly.

Some states refused to ratify the Constitution until the delegates agreed to include a Bill of Rights. Such a bill would outline a list of the basic rights guaranteed to U.S.

Each year, the president of the United States delivers a State of the Union address before both houses of Congress.

citizens. These rights could never be taken away by the government. With the Bill of Rights promised to be on the way, all 13 states ratified the Constitution by May 1790.

A FIRSTHAND LOOK AT
THE CONSTITUTION OF THE UNITED STATES

On September 17, 1787, 39 of the 55 delegates at the Constitutional Convention signed in support of the document they had created. The Constitution outlines the basic structure, powers, and responsibilities of the U.S. government. See page 60 for a link to view it online.

A Land of Freedoms

The delegates to the Constitutional Convention had created a process for making amendments, or changes, to the U.S. Constitution. In 1791, the first 10 amendments were added to the Constitution as the Bill of Rights. These 10 amendments guarantee certain rights to all U.S. citizens. For example, the First Amendment guarantees free speech, freedom of the press, and freedom of religion. Free speech enables people to openly express their thoughts about government policies. Freedom of the press protects the work of journalists from government **censorship**. Such freedoms ensure that people in the

The more than 13,000 newspapers published in the United States are all protected from government interference by the First Amendment.

United States can help spread the information that others need to make informed opinions at the voting booth.

Though the Constitution and the Bill of Rights were created hundreds of years ago, they continue to have an effect on the modern world. For example, the First Amendment's guarantees of free speech and a free press allow the country's people to freely spread information over the Internet. Though the Founding Fathers could not have envisioned the technology of the 21st century, they created a Constitution that could be interpreted in ways that would preserve American freedoms for all time.

TODAY'S PERSPECTIVE

While freedom of speech and freedom of the press are guaranteed in the United States, other governments do not allow their people to openly discuss certain political opinions. The Iranian government filters the Internet, blocking access to many Web sites. Many Iranian citizens have objected by using special Internet connections called virtual private networks (VPNs) to avoid the filters. In response, Iran's leaders have outlawed all VPNs that are not registered with the government. This permits Iranian officials to monitor Internet use. Officials may soon make it impossible for Iranian citizens to access the Internet at all.

CHAPTER 2

OTHER FORMS OF GOVERNMENT

Like the U.S. Congress, the United Kingdom's Parliament is divided into two houses and has the power to change or create laws.

THERE ARE NEARLY 200

countries in the world today. Each of these nations has a unique government. Some governments are similar to that of the United States. Others are remarkably different. Instead of allowing people to choose their own leaders, some systems of government have a single ruler who holds total power.

Governments can exist for very different reasons and serve very different purposes. Some are the product of hundreds of years of history and tradition. Others have been formed in more recent years. But no matter their structure or style of ruling, all governments have a huge effect on the lives of their countries' people.

Under the leadership of Kim Jong-il (right), the North Korean government was accused of significant human rights violations.

Government in North Korea

In some countries, rulers govern without the people's consent. Such countries are often led by a single individual or committee that holds absolute power. The people do not choose these dictators in elections. Instead, dictators usually inherit power through their families or seize control of the government through military force.

Founded in 1948, North Korea is a dictatorship that was first led by a ruler named Kim Il-sung. When Kim Il-sung died in 1994, he was succeeded by his son, Kim Jong-il. While the Kims lived in luxury, nearly half of North Korea's young children struggled to get enough to eat. More than 200,000 prisoners were forced to work in harsh labor camps. Many of these people were tortured and starved. In addition, Kim Jong-il's government carefully monitored all communication, including mail and telephone calls. Only **Communist** Party insiders were allowed to use the Internet.

When Kim Jong-il died in 2011, he was succeeded by his son, Kim Jong-un. Kim Jong-un has continued his father's policies, making military strength a state priority. The state also maintains tight control over all media and limits the people's contact with foreign visitors. In addition, North Korea's official news agency censors all news entering the country. As a result, the people of North Korea know very little about the world outside their home country.

Kim Jong-un (front, center) is the world's youngest leader of a national government.

The Cuban Government

Cuba is another country where the Communist Party controls the government without competition from other parties. Censorship is widespread in Cuba. The government owns all media outlets. The Cuban constitution specifically grants the Communist Party the right to regulate the press. Cuba's news is carried on state-sponsored radio and television, and is printed in Communist Party newspapers owned by the government. Journalists are often jailed for expressing ideas the government disagrees with.

Until recently, cell phones were extremely rare in Cuba. Anyone who wanted a phone line had to

The current president of Cuba, Raúl Castro (left), is the brother of former president Fidel Castro (right), who led the nation for almost 50 years.

be screened and approved by the government. Most applications were denied. Getting Internet access requires state approval in Cuba, too. People who connect to the Internet without approval can be jailed for years. It is also illegal to purchase a computer without approval from the government.

Cuba has many laws to prevent its people from speaking out against the government. Individuals the state labels as dangerous, including nonviolent political opponents, can be placed under police observation or put in mental hospitals. If more than two people work together to demonstrate against the government, they can be jailed. People arrested for opposing the government are routinely denied fair trials. The government is not even required to inform these people of the charges brought against them.

Laws also restrict the movement of Cuban citizens. Government approval is necessary to leave the island. In 1994, when 72 Cubans tried to leave from Havana on a tugboat, government ships sank the tugboat. Forty-one people drowned in the attack, including several children.

Communist Economies

Vietnam, Laos, and China are also Communist states. During the 20th century, Communist states such as China and the former Soviet Union had planned economies. This means the government made decisions about how resources would be used and what would be produced. It set prices and made investments that would benefit the state. By the 1980s, some

In China, Internet companies are required to report users who violate the country's strict Internet laws.

Communist states began to hand over limited economic control to privately owned companies. Today, Cuba and North Korea still have fully planned economies. Laos and China have mixed economies.

This slight loosening of economic control has allowed China's economy to grow rapidly. However, the Communist Party still wields political power and censors media reports on a wide variety of topics. Public discussions of religion, food safety, and **democracy** are all prohibited. The government restricts access to the Internet, including Facebook and YouTube. Newspapers, radio, television, and even video games are censored.

Governed by Religion

Theocracies are governments that are based on religious beliefs. For example, nations such as Iran and Saudi Arabia base their beliefs on the version of Islam their leaders believe in. These countries' laws are subject to interpretation by religious courts.

In Iran, an Islamic scholar called the Supreme Leader is even more powerful than the president. His approval is needed for important appointments to the military and the courts. He himself is appointed by other Islamic scholars. Even though Iran's constitution

YESTERDAY'S HEADLINES

In the spring of 1989, students led a street protest in Beijing, China's capital city. They hoped to bring democracy to the country. Huge crowds of protesters occupied Beijing's Tiananmen Square (above) for seven weeks. The Communist Party eventually sent tanks and troops armed with assault rifles to break up the demonstration. Many protesters were killed during the crackdown.

In the aftermath, the Chinese government removed from office those officials who had sympathized with the Tiananmen Square demonstrators. Media censorship increased, and foreign journalists were sent home. Today, the Chinese government has outlawed public mention of the Tiananmen Square massacre.

A FIRSTHAND LOOK AT
THE CONSTITUTION OF THE ISLAMIC REPUBLIC OF IRAN

The Iranian government is both a republic and a theocracy. While Iran's citizens elect many of the government's leaders, they are required to live under religious laws. See page 60 for a link to read Iran's constitution online.

contains some democratic principles, and the country is considered an Islamic republic, the Supreme Leader is the ultimate source of power and social order.

Unlike Iran, Saudi Arabia is led by a king, rather than elected officials. However, both nations are governed by religious law. In Saudi Arabia, Islamic law is enforced by religious police known as the *mutaween*. The mutaween uphold the state's conservative beliefs. They make sure citizens obey the government's interpretation of the rules

The Saudi Arabian religious police, or mutaween, are officially known as the Committee for the Promotion of Virtue and Prevention of Vice.

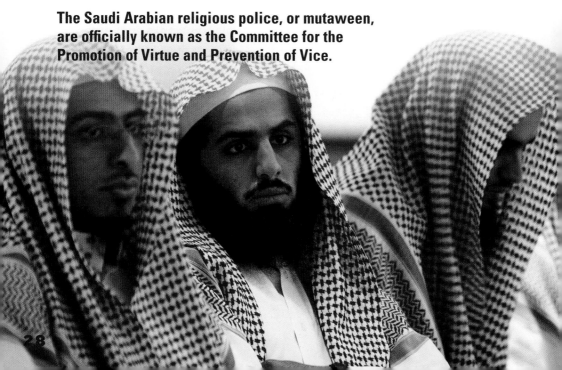

Elizabeth II has been the queen of England since 1952.

of the Qur'an, Islam's holy book. They are charged with enforcing dietary laws and dress codes. In 2002, the mutaween stopped several girls trying to escape from a burning school building in Mecca because the students were not wearing the required black robes and head scarves. Critics around the globe were outraged.

The mutaween also work to stamp out cultural influences from American and European nations. They seize music CDs and routinely arrest anyone practicing religions other than Islam. For example, 40 Christians were arrested in 2005 for trying to convert Saudis to Christianity.

Kings and Queens

In a monarchy, a king or queen wields power over the entire government. That power is passed along through the royal family. Once in power, a monarch usually rules for life. As recently as the 19th century, traditional

monarchies were a common form of government.

Today, most monarchies work differently than they once did. Most common is the constitutional monarchy. In a constitutional monarchy, the monarch shares power with a second source of authority established by the nation's constitution. With the exception of Vatican City, all of modern Europe's monarchies are constitutional.

The amount of power a constitutional monarch possesses varies a great deal from one nation to another. In many European monarchies, the monarch's role is almost entirely ceremonial. In others, such as

Liechtenstein, the monarch's power is nearly absolute. He can dismiss elected government officials or reject any law proposed by Liechtenstein's legislature. The only check on his power is that the people can call for his removal.

Some monarchies do not fit neatly into categories. For example, Vatican City and Swaziland are both absolute monarchies. However, they have very different leadership. The pope, who is the leader of the Roman Catholic Church, also serves as the monarch of Vatican City. Meanwhile, Swaziland is ruled by two monarchs. The king and his mother are both heads of state. Each is meant to check the power of the other, and their roles complement each other. Even within a single form of government, there are many variations in the distribution of power, depending on the country.

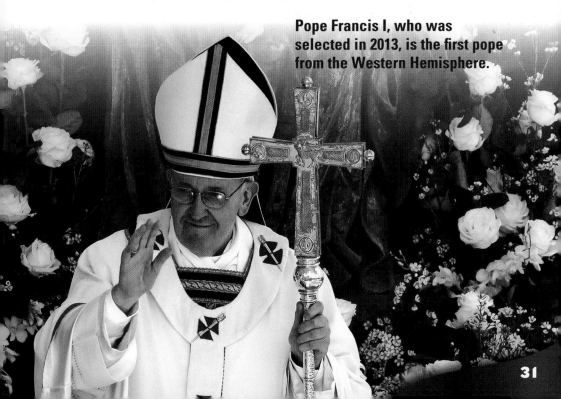

Pope Francis I, who was selected in 2013, is the first pope from the Western Hemisphere.

CHAPTER 3

NATION TO NATION

After many years of unresolved conflict, the United States invaded Iraq in 2003 to remove Iraqi president Saddam Hussein from power.

DIFFERENCES IN HOW NATIONS are governed and their stances on controversial issues occasionally bring them into conflict with one another. A government's policies on nuclear weapons, human rights, climate change, or the global economy can create tension among nations that have different aims. In the past century, governments have resolved those tensions in a variety of ways. Sometimes conflicts are solved when nations can come to a fair agreement. Other times, one country might use the threat of military force or economic pressure to get what it wants. Sometimes, the only solution is warfare. Such conflicts have marked some of the most significant events in history, and they continue to do so today.

Hot and Cold

Sometimes, governments interact violently. Beginning in 1931, Japan waged war to gain control of China's vast resources. By 1937, Japan had launched a full-scale invasion of mainland China. Fearing the expansion of Japan and its growing military power, the United States, the United Kingdom, and France began providing assistance to China. They also communicated with Japan in an effort to find a peaceful end to the conflict. By September 1940, Japan had expanded into what is now northern Vietnam, Laos, and Cambodia.

Japan's invasion of China during the mid-20th century is known as the Second Sino-Japanese War.

On December 7, 1941, Japan launched a surprise attack on the U.S. naval base at Pearl Harbor, Hawaii. The attack forced the hand of the United States. Diplomacy had failed, and the American public now clamored for revenge. The United States was thrust into World War II (1939–1945) against Japan and its allies in Germany and Italy.

After the war ended in 1945, several nations cooperated to form the United Nations. This organization aims to prevent large conflicts such as World War II. It promotes peace, economic development, and human rights worldwide.

War is sometimes the result of failed diplomacy. Other times, it is used to achieve larger strategic objectives. The United States' involvement in the Vietnam War (1954–1975) was part of a larger plan to combat the spread of

The United Nations

The United Nations was formed in 1945, in the wake of the devastation of World War II. Upon the organization's formation, 51 countries around the world agreed to participate. Today, more than 190 nations are members. Originally established to promote world peace, the United Nations' activities are now far reaching. Recognizing the connection between larger social problems and maintaining peace, the organization now plays an active role in public health, international justice, hunger relief, and climate change, among other issues. Its headquarters is located in New York City.

The Soviet satellite *Sputnik 1* was the first manufactured satellite ever to orbit Earth.

Communism. The Soviet Union and China provided military assistance to the Communist government in North Vietnam. As a result, the United States gradually found it necessary to increase its role in Vietnam to contain Communism. The United States and the Soviet Union did not declare war on each other. Instead, the governments of North and South Vietnam became stand-ins in a larger international struggle between the two superpowers.

Though the United States and the Soviet Union did not engage in conventional warfare, the two nations worked constantly to influence each other and shape public opinion. Between 1947 and 1991, the two superpowers vied for supremacy in ways that were both aggressive and peaceful. This period of nonviolent interaction is known as the Cold War. During the Cold War, the two nations spied on each other, stockpiled nuclear weapons, and competed for Olympic medals. They also raced to determine which would be the first country with a successful space program.

Tensions occasionally flared up during the Cold War, making open warfare seem likely. In April 1961, U.S. president John F. Kennedy approved a plan to invade Cuba and overthrow its Communist government. The

The Cuban Missile Crisis ended when Soviet leader Nikita Khrushchev (left) agreed to remove nuclear missiles from Cuba, and President John F. Kennedy (right) agreed that the United States would never invade Cuba.

plot failed. In response, the Soviet Union placed nuclear missiles in Cuba to deter another attack from the United States. When U.S. spy photos revealed the military buildup in 1962, Kennedy and Soviet leader Nikita Khrushchev entered into tense negotiations to avoid nuclear war. Nations will usually seek peaceful solutions when tensions rise. They have learned from past events that they often gain more from diplomacy than warfare.

Working Together

Governments often use diplomacy to find common ground. In 1978, U.S. president Jimmy Carter brought together leaders and diplomats from Egypt and Israel at

President Jimmy Carter (center) met with Egyptian president Anwar Sadat (left) and Israeli prime minister Menachem Begin (right) to create an agreement officially called the Framework for Peace in the Middle East, more commonly known as the Camp David Accords.

Camp David, north of Washington, D.C. Tensions had been building between the two nations for 30 years. In 1967, Israel had seized control of the Sinai Peninsula from Egypt. Thereafter, the Sinai Peninsula became the site of military confrontations between Israel and Egypt. The two nations also contended for control of important waterways. Carter worked tirelessly with the two leaders and their diplomats to build an agreement. Thanks to these negotiations, Egypt and Israel developed an ongoing process to bring peace to the region.

A VIEW FROM ABROAD

In an effort to stop the spread of nuclear weapons, the United Nations Security Council has in recent years issued a series of **resolutions** aimed at regulating Iran's nuclear program. Iran's government has argued that it is working to expand peacetime use of nuclear energy. However, without regulation, the same programs could be used to make nuclear weapons.

When one of the resolutions was brought to a vote before the Security Council in 2010, 12 of the council's 15 members supported it. However, leaders in Brazil and Turkey argued that the resolutions were not achieving their goal. They have pushed instead for patient diplomacy. They believe that trying to win Iran's cooperation is a better way forward. Though United Nations resolutions aim to find agreement among nations, they sometimes reveal the differences among governments.

Nations often act together to protect common interests. For example, use of nuclear weapons is a threat to all nations. Beginning in 2006, the United Nations Security Council adopted a series of resolutions forbidding the development of nuclear weapons in Iran. Resolution 1929 was passed in June 2010. It extended an existing **embargo** on selling arms and military technology to Iran. It also sought the cooperation of member nations in cutting funding for Iran's activities.

Diplomacy and Economics

Other times, one nation will apply economic pressure on another to get that nation to change its policies. After Cuba's 1959 Communist **revolution**, new leader Fidel Castro and his government began to take over privately owned U.S. companies based in Cuba. The U.S. government fought back when Cuba failed to make fair payment to those companies. It placed a trade embargo on Cuba in 1960 and strengthened it two years later. The embargo has remained in place for more than 50 years. Today, the United States does not engage in trade with Cuba.

Sometimes, economic pressure can bring big changes to the way a country is governed. The government of South Africa once supported a system of apartheid. Under this system, black people were treated unfairly and forced to live in designated areas away from white people. In 1986, the U.S. Congress passed the Comprehensive Anti-Apartheid Act. It was intended to

A FIRSTHAND LOOK AT
THE CUBAN DEMOCRACY ACT OF 1992

The Cuban Democracy Act of 1992 was designed to extend the U.S. embargo on Cuba and encourage U.S. trading partners to limit their economic support of Cuba. Its ultimate goal is the replacement of Cuba's Communist government with a free democratic system. See page 60 for a link to read the act online.

force the South African government to end apartheid. Under the act, the United States reduced trade with South Africa and banned new investment in the country. This economic pressure helped persuade South Africa to end the racial discrimination of apartheid.

Under apartheid, many buildings, public areas, and even benches were made off-limits to black South Africans.

CHAPTER 4

MAKING CHANGES

Members of the U.S. Congress debate their ideas and make compromises as they work to ensure that the nation's laws reflect voters' wishes.

EACH NATION HAS A FORM OF government that has arisen from its unique history and reflects its society's values. However, new technologies and new perspectives on old problems can lead to major changes in societies. As the expectations of citizens and the opinions of other nations evolve, governments are often forced to adapt their policies. Sometimes, existing governments are even removed from power completely and replaced with new systems.

The president regularly meets with his cabinet to receive trusted advice on a variety of issues concerning the country.

A Growing Government

The U.S. government has changed in many ways since it was founded more than 225 years ago. For example, the balance of power among the three branches has shifted. The executive branch, especially the Office of the President, did not possess the wide-ranging powers it now does. In addition, the influence of the Supreme Court has grown.

The size and complexity of the federal government has also grown. The first president, George Washington, appointed four men to advise him. Today, President Obama's cabinet of advisers has 15 departments with far-reaching powers. The cabinet has sometimes been enlarged in response to emerging problems. After the

A FIRSTHAND LOOK AT
THE HOMELAND SECURITY ACT OF 2002

The Homeland Security Act was approved in the aftermath of the terrorist attacks of September 11, 2001. It reorganized existing governmental programs such as the Coast Guard, the Secret Service, and the U.S. Customs Service. This reorganization made these groups better able to act together in the event of terrorist acts. See page 60 for a link to view the act online.

terrorist attacks of September 11, 2001, the Department of Homeland Security was created to ensure the safety of U.S. citizens. Despite the growth of the cabinet, all officers are still appointed by the president and then either confirmed or rejected by a vote in the Senate.

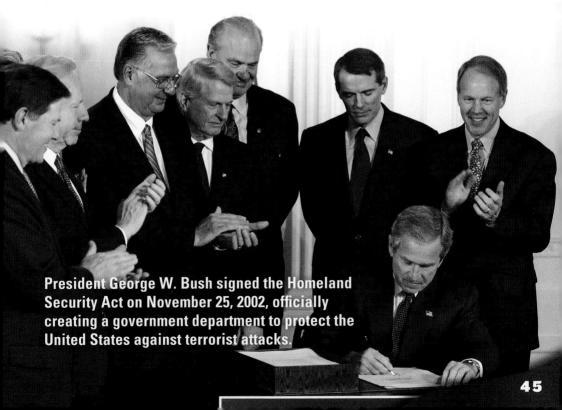

President George W. Bush signed the Homeland Security Act on November 25, 2002, officially creating a government department to protect the United States against terrorist attacks.

Changes at Home

A process for changing the U.S. Constitution was built into the document during its creation. Article V states that a new amendment must be approved by a two-thirds vote in each house of Congress. Once approved, it is sent to state legislatures. Three-fourths of the states must ratify the amendment for it to be adopted. Thousands of proposed amendments have been put before Congress. Only 27 of them have received congressional approval and been ratified by state legislatures.

Six of the 15 amendments approved since the Civil War (1861–1865) have dealt with voting rights. Before the Constitution was ratified, many states allowed only white, land-owning males to vote. Native Americans, African

The U.S. government allowed segregation for many years before the Supreme Court's 1954 ruling in *Brown v. Board of Education*.

COLORED
WAITING ROOM

PRIVATE PROPERTY
NO PARKING
Driving through or Turning Around

BINGO
TONITE!

Good
Housekeeping

True Story
HITLER'S
LOVE LIFE
REVEALED

CAROLINA COACH COMPANY   45

Americans, and women were excluded. In 1870, the 15th Amendment banned voting restrictions based on race. In 1920, the 19th Amendment gave women the right to vote.

The federal government also responds to social change through Supreme Court rulings. In 1896, the court ruled in favor of racial segregation in *Plessy v. Ferguson*. It declared that separating black and white people was legal as long as they were provided with equal facilities and opportunities. In reality, equality was seldom achieved. Across the South, racial discrimination

TODAY'S PERSPECTIVE

In 1920, the passage of the 19th Amendment gave women the right to vote. However, women began fighting to gain voting rights in the mid-1800s. Slowly, they began to achieve success at the state level. After the Civil War, activists were disappointed by the 15th Amendment, which extended voting rights to men of all races. They had hoped that its scope would be widened to include women. Instead, women battled for another half century before winning the right to vote.

Today, it is difficult to image a time when women were not allowed to participate in government. Women play a major role in elections, and in recent years many of the nation's top offices have been filled by women.

The *Brown v. Board of Education* case began when Oliver Brown (right) sued the Board of Education of Topeka, Kansas, to allow his daughter Linda (left) to attend a white-only school that was near the family's home.

was rampant. African Americans had inferior schools and fewer employment opportunities. In 1954, the Supreme Court reviewed the issue of school segregation in *Brown v. Board of Education*. The court's ruling struck down the standard of "separate but equal" facilities.

Congress can make changes to the way the nation is governed by passing new laws. For example, a decade after the *Brown v. Board of Education* decision, Congress passed the Civil Rights Act of 1964. This act brought the country one step closer to ending racial inequality.

Revolution

Governments sometimes change in response to events in other countries. During the 1980s, political unrest spread throughout Eastern Europe. In several countries, citizens grew frustrated with sluggish economies and Communist leadership. When Mikhail Gorbachev came to power in the Soviet Union in 1985, he loosened government control of the economy. People in neighboring Communist countries were encouraged by these changes. They began protesting their own governments in the hope of making changes similar to the ones in the Soviet Union. In 1989, Romanians overthrew their government and replaced it with a republic.

More than 1,000 protesters were killed in the 1989 Romanian revolution.

Mikhail Gorbachev

When Mikhail Gorbachev assumed leadership of the Soviet Union's Communist Party in 1985, his nation's economy was suffering. Gorbachev immediately launched the nation on the path of reform. He streamlined the government to make it more efficient. He also supported faster technological progress and greater agricultural productivity. He soon came to understand that these changes were not enough. It would be necessary to overhaul the government entirely. Gorbachev spoke in favor of democratic reforms. By improving relations with Western nations, he paved the way for further reform and the end of the Soviet Union and the Cold War. His quiet revolution changed the world forever.

A similar wave of revolutionary efforts began in December 2010, when riots and civil wars swept through the Arab world with incredible speed. Protesters demonstrated against government corruption, weak economies, and high rates of unemployment.

More than a dozen countries were affected by the protests, and leaders were removed from power in four nations. Demonstrators used social media to organize the uprisings. In Egypt, the government responded by shutting down the Internet for five days in January 2011. Libya's government imposed an Internet curfew the following month in an attempt to end the protests. The leaders of both countries were soon forced from power.

In early 2011, protesters gathered in Tahrir Square in Cairo, Egypt, to celebrate the resignation of Egyptian president Hosni Mubarak.

In Egypt, president Hosni Mubarak was replaced by a new president, Mohamed Morsi, who was elected in 2012. Soon after taking office, Morsi began granting himself more power over the country's government. Once again, Egypt's people rose in protest against their leader. In 2013, Morsi was removed from office by the Egyptian military. The military will control the country's government until a new election can be held.

The protests of 1989 and 2010–2011 have much in common. The citizens shared in similar frustrations, including economic failure, a lack of opportunity, and corruption. Governments that ignore the will of the people and fail to represent their interests do so at their own peril. Eventually, they may be swept from power and replaced.

MAP OF THE EVENTS
What Happened Where?

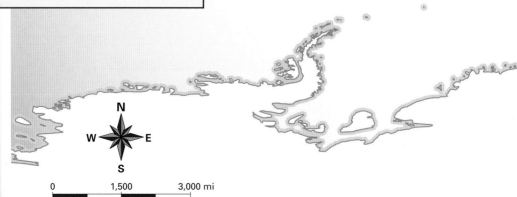

UNITED STATES

⊛ Washington, D.C.

Pearl Harbor

Havana ⊛

CUBA

ATLANTIC OCEAN

Pearl Harbor, Hawaii, USA
On December 7, 1941, Japanese forces attacked the U.S. naval base at Pearl Harbor. This attack drew the United States into World War II.

Havana, Cuba
Havana is the capital city of Cuba. Here, Fidel Castro and his brother Raúl have ruled the nation as a Communist government since 1959.

N
W ✦ E
S

0   1,500   3,000 mi
0   1,500   3,000 km

ARCTIC OCEAN

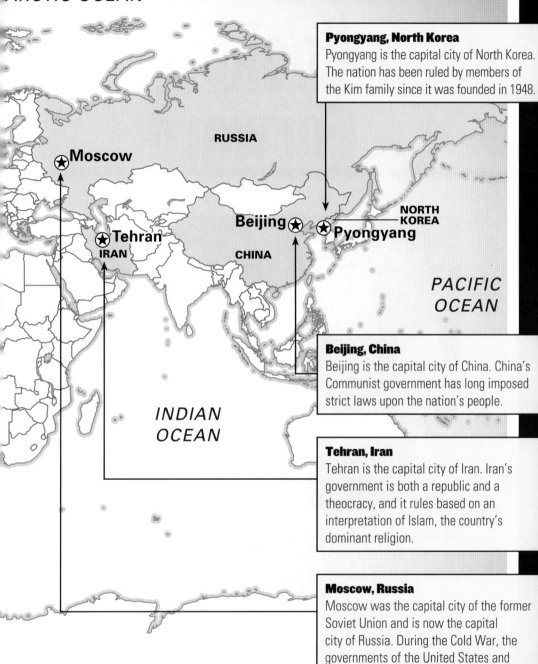

RUSSIA

Moscow

Tehran

IRAN

Beijing

CHINA

NORTH
KOREA

Pyongyang

PACIFIC
OCEAN

INDIAN
OCEAN

Pyongyang, North Korea
Pyongyang is the capital city of North Korea.
The nation has been ruled by members of
the Kim family since it was founded in 1948.

Beijing, China
Beijing is the capital city of China. China's
Communist government has long imposed
strict laws upon the nation's people.

Tehran, Iran
Tehran is the capital city of Iran. Iran's
government is both a republic and a
theocracy, and it rules based on an
interpretation of Islam, the country's
dominant religion.

Moscow, Russia
Moscow was the capital city of the former
Soviet Union and is now the capital
city of Russia. During the Cold War, the
governments of the United States and
the Soviet Union had a tense, competitive
relationship.

Looking Forward

Internet access through smartphones, tablet computers, and other portable devices makes it possible for people to learn about events as they are unfolding almost anywhere in the world.

The challenges governments face in the future will require them to continue to adapt. More than ever before, the Internet and the growing ease of travel will remove

MORE THAN I BILLION PEOPLE AROUND

barriers to communication. Nations with very different economies and political beliefs will be required to cooperate with one another in a global marketplace. This will continue to create friction even as opportunity grows.

Governments will also face common problems. They will have to respond to and protect citizens from terrorist acts. They will have to devise plans to cope with changes brought by environmental change. Citizens everywhere will demand a greater voice in decision making. It has never been more important for citizens to understand their own government and governments of other nations.

Governments around the world are trying to find the balance between the need for energy sources and the need to prevent damage to the natural world.

THE WORLD USE SMARTPHONES TODAY.

INFLUENTIAL INDIVIDUALS

James Madison

James Madison (1751–1836) was a Virginia delegate to the Constitutional Convention who supported a strong federal government. Known as the Father of the Constitution, he later served as the fourth president of the United States.

Nikita Khrushchev (1894–1971) was the premier of the Soviet Union from 1958 to 1964. His decision to install nuclear missiles in Cuba led to the Cuban Missile Crisis during the Cold War.

Fidel Castro (1926–) was the Communist leader who seized control of Cuba in 1959. For health reasons, he handed over control of the country to his brother Raúl in 2008.

Fidel Castro

John F. Kennedy (1917–1963) was the 35th president of the United States. He successfully led the nation through the Cuban Missile Crisis during the Cold War.

Jimmy Carter (1924–) was the 39th president of the United States. He was the architect of the Camp David Accords, agreements that helped create peace between Egypt and Israel.

Mikhail Gorbachev (1931–) was the leader of the Soviet Union's Communist Party from 1985 to 1991. He worked to lessen economic restrictions and bring democracy to his country, leading to the end of the Soviet Union in 1991.

Mikhail Gorbachev

Kim Jong-un (ca. 1983–) is the Communist leader of North Korea. He assumed power in 2011 upon the death of his father, Kim Jong-il.

TIMELINE

1774

The First Continental Congress meets.

1776

The Second Continental Congress issues the Declaration of Independence.

1781

The Articles of Confederation go into effect.

1870

The 15th Amendment to the Constitution is ratified.

1920

The 19th Amendment to the Constitution is ratified.

1941

December 7
The Japanese attack on Pearl Harbor draws the United States into World War II.

1945

The United Nations is formed.

1960–Present

The United States maintains a trade embargo on Cuba.

1985

Mikhail Gorbachev comes to power in the Soviet Union.

1989

A series of revolutions brings new governments to Eastern Europe; student protesters in Tiananmen Square attempt to bring democracy to China.

1787

May–September
The Constitutional Convention is held to set up a government.

1790

The U.S. Constitution is ratified.

1791

The Bill of Rights is adopted.

1947–1991

The Cold War is waged between the United States and the Soviet Union.

1954

The Supreme Court rules on *Brown v. Board of Education*.

1959

Fidel Castro seizes power in Cuba.

1992

The Cuban Democracy Act is signed.

2010

Resolution 1929 is approved by the UN Security Council.

2010–2013

The Arab Spring protests lead to civil wars and revolutions in the Middle East.

LIVING HISTORY

Primary sources provide firsthand evidence about a topic. Witnesses to a historical event create primary sources. They include autobiographies, newspaper reports of the time, oral histories, photographs, and memoirs. A secondary source analyzes primary sources, and is one step or more removed from the event. Secondary sources include textbooks, encyclopedias, and commentaries. To view the following primary and secondary sources, go to www.factsfornow .scholastic.com. Enter the keywords **Forms of Government** and look for the Living History logo ⵢ.

ⵢ The Constitution of the Islamic Republic of Iran Iran's constitution serves a government that is both a republic and a theocracy. While Iranian citizens elect many of the government's leaders, they are required to live under religious laws. You can read a copy of Iran's constitution online.

ⵢ The Constitution of the United States The United States Constitution is the founding document of the nation's government. Though it has been amended and reinterpreted throughout the country's history, the original document still stands as the backbone of the United States government.

ⵢ The Cuban Democracy Act of 1992 The Cuban Democracy Act of 1992 was designed to extend the U.S. embargo on Cuba and encourage U.S. trading partners to limit their economic support of Cuba. You can read a copy of the act online.

ⵢ The Homeland Security Act of 2002 The Homeland Security Act was approved in the aftermath of the terrorist attacks of September 11, 2001. It reorganized existing governmental programs to make them better able to act together in the event of other terrorist acts. You can read the text of the act online.

RESOURCES

Books

Burgan, Michael. *The U.S. Constitution*. New York: Children's Press, 2012.

McDaniel, Melissa. *The Declaration of Independence*. New York: Children's Press, 2012.

Raatma, Lucia. *The Bill of Rights*. New York: Children's Press, 2012.

Visit this Scholastic Web site for more information on the forms of government: www.factsfornow.scholastic.com Enter the keywords Forms of Government

GLOSSARY

censorship (SEN-sur-ship) the removal of ideas and information that are thought to be unacceptable or offensive

colonies (KAH-luh-neez) territories that have been settled by people from another country and are controlled by that country

communist (KAHM-yuh-nist) describing a way of organizing the economy of a country so that all land, property, businesses, and resources belong to the government or community, and the profits are shared by all

constitution (kahn-stuh-TOO-shuhn) the basic laws of a country that state the rights of the people and the powers of the government

delegates (DEL-i-guts) people who represent a larger group of people at a meeting

democracy (di-MAH-kruh-see) a form of government in which people choose their leaders in elections

diplomacy (dip-LOH-muh-see) negotiation between governments

economies (i-KAHN-uh-meez) the systems of buying, selling, making things, and managing money in a place

embargo (em-BAR-go) an official order forbidding something from happening, especially trade

legislature (LEJ-uss-lay-chur) the part of government that is responsible for making and changing laws

ratification (rat-uh-fi-KAY-shuhn) the process of agreeing or approving officially

resolutions (rez-uh-LOO-shuhnz) formal expressions of opinion, will, or intent voted on by an official body or assembled group

revolution (rev-uh-LOO-shuhn) a violent overthrow of a country's government or ruler by the people who live there

Page numbers in *italics* indicate illustrations.

ABOUT THE AUTHOR

Peter Benoit is the author of more than 50 books. He has written about ecosystems, Native Americans, disasters, ancient civilizations, and numerous topics in American history. Benoit is a graduate of Skidmore College. He lives in Greenwich, New York.